21 Day HOLY CHICKS DEVOTIONAL

CHRYSTAL JOHNSON

BookLeaf Publishing

India | USA | UK

Presentation by *BookLeaf Publishing*

Web: www.bookleafpub.com
E-mail: info@bookleafpub.com

ISBN: 9789369538577

First edition 2025

Dedication

This devotional is lovingly dedicated to every woman who has ever questioned her worth, doubted her calling, or struggled to rise after a fall. To the daughters, sisters, mothers, and warriors who desire to walk in holiness but feel the weight of their past—know this: you are not disqualified. You are deeply loved, chosen, and called for such a time as this.

To the women of all ages and all stages, may this devotional be a gentle reminder that holiness is not out of reach. It is a daily decision, a heart posture, and a beautiful journey into deeper intimacy with Jesus (Yeshua).

To my precious baby boy, Cadence, whose life, though brief, changed mine forever. Your passing broke something deep within me, but it also birthed a new level of surrender, purpose, and fire in my walk with God. Your name means rhythm, and though the beat of my life shifted the day you left, I carry your rhythm in every prayer, every tear, every testimony, and every word written here. You made me stronger. You made me softer. You made me holier.

To every Holy Chick rising—this is for you. Come out from among them. Be set apart. Be refined. And walk boldly into the holy life God has prepared for you. Even in your pain, purpose is waiting. Even in your process, He is present.

With all my love and devotion,
Chrystal Johnson

holy
chicks
titus 2:3-5

PREFACE

This 21-day Holy Chicks Devotional was birthed from a deep place of surrender, sanctification, and unwavering love for the women of God—women of all ages, from every walk of life—who desire to walk in holiness, be set apart, and live a life fully submitted to the Lord. This devotional is not just a daily read; it's a spiritual journey—a call to return to the feet of Jesus (Yeshua), to grow in grace, truth, and fire-tested faith.

Though I've walked with God my entire life, it wasn't until I was about 22 years old that I truly surrendered and began living a life set apart for Him. Through seasons of trials, loss, and testing, God has consistently revealed His faithfulness. I've faced the unimaginable—including the death of my child—a pain that shook my faith, but also refined it. It was in that crushing that I discovered the true meaning of being anchored in Jesus (Yeshua).

When I turned 40, I fell into sin—a fall that humbled me and showed me how easy it is to drift, even after years of strong faith. But it was also a necessary fall. God used that season to break the spirit of self-righteousness and pride in me. I came back to Him, not just with tears, but with repentance and a renewed commitment. I rededicated my life and was baptized again as an adult, and from that moment on, I understood the importance of hearing God's voice, obeying without delay, and walking in holiness—not perfection, but daily consecration.

This devotional walks you through topics such as repentance, prayer, deliverance, obedience, identity, spiritual warfare, and healing. It's raw. It's real. It's personal. And it's anchored in the Word of God.

My heart is for every woman reading this to know: you're not alone. Holiness is still possible. Sanctification is still relevant. And even when your faith is tested, you can stand firm. This is your invitation to live set apart—holy, healed, and wholly His.

Let's walk this out—together.

In His Love,
Chrystal Johnson

"The aged women likewise, that they be in behaviour as becometh holiness, not false accusers, not given to much wine, teachers of good things; That they may teach the young women to be sober, to love their husbands, to love their children, To be discreet, chaste, keepers at home, good, obedient to their own husbands, that the word of God be not blasphemed."

— Titus 2:3–5 (KJV)

"Follow peace with all men, and holiness, without which no man shall see the Lord:"

— Hebrews 12:14 (KJV)

INTRODUCTION: REPENTANCE

"If we confess our sins, He is faithful and just to forgive and cleanse us from all unrighteousness."

— 1 John 1:9

Repentance is not just a ritual—it's a life-changing practice that opens the door for spiritual renewal, healing, and transformation. It's not always easy, especially when we've been through pain, loss, or personal struggle, but it's essential for our growth in God. It's the first step in aligning our hearts with His will, helping us break free from the grip of sin, and guiding us toward a life of purpose and spiritual freedom.

Repentance matters because we are all imperfect; we all fall short. Life's hardships and the weight of our mistakes can make us feel far from God, but repentance is the way back to Him. It's not just about being sorry for what we've done—it's about turning away from the patterns of sin that hold us back and asking God to cleanse, heal, and restore us. Through the Holy Spirit, we can break the chains of sin, bondage, and generational curses that may have kept us stuck for years.

"For all have sinned and fall short of the glory of God."

— Romans 3:23

This doesn't mean we are beyond hope—God has already made a way for us. His grace is more significant than our failures. But we must acknowledge where we have fallen short, confess it, and lean on God for the strength to turn away from it. Only through His Spirit can we walk a righteous path.

In my own life, I've seen how repentance can be a breakthrough moment. When things felt impossible, when pain weighed on me, when life didn't make sense, I felt the most strength in those moments of surrender. In turning to God, acknowledging my failures, and seeking His help, I found forgiveness and a deeper connection with Him. Through that connection,

I was able to start walking a new path, one of healing and restoration, with Him leading me.

"I am the Vine; you are the branches. The one who remains in Me and I in him bears much fruit, for apart from Me, you can do nothing."
— John 15:5

Repentance is more than admitting wrong; it's about seeking God's help to turn away from sin and overcome the things that keep us from being who He created us to be. It's about humbling ourselves and allowing God's love to transform us from the inside out. With His guidance, we are given the strength to break free from destructive patterns and walk in righteousness.

God's love is our strength. His grace empowers us to live in freedom, walk in holiness, and be who we were meant to be. But it begins with repentance—a heartfelt desire to change, to live for Him, and to embrace His healing power.

Today, I invite you to examine your heart. Reflect on your thoughts, actions, and words—ask yourself, "Where have I missed the mark?" Be transparent with God. Hold nothing back. Repent with sincerity, knowing His arms are open wide, ready to receive, cleanse, and restore you to a place of peace and purpose.

PRAYER:

Lord, I come before You today with a heart of repentance. I acknowledge the areas where I have fallen short, sinned, or strayed away from Your will. I ask for Your forgiveness and cleansing, knowing You are faithful to forgive and renew me. Help me turn away from the things that hinder my walk with You, and guide me in Your righteousness. I invite Your Spirit to strengthen me and transform my heart so I may live a life of holiness and purpose, walking closely with You. Thank You for Your grace, Your love, and Your faithfulness.

In Yeshua's Name (Jesus), HalleluYah and it is so !

REFLECTION QUESTIONS:

- Where do you need to repent and seek God's forgiveness today?
- What patterns of sin or habits do you need to release and ask God to help you overcome?
- How can you stay accountable to your commitment to holiness and purpose in Christ?

Repentance is not a burden; it is a pathway to freedom. God is eagerly waiting to help you walk a new path today.

JOURNALING:

DEVOTIONAL: PRAYER

Communing with God is an intimate and powerful way to connect with our Heavenly Father, allowing us to share our thoughts, feelings, and desires. Through prayer, we can experience profound healing, transformation, and guidance as we align our lives with God's loving will. Prayer is our communication with Our Father, God, and we should pray constantly and consistently. By prioritizing prayer, we cultivate a more profound sense of trust, peace, and purpose, enabling us to live more authentically, confidently, and compassionately.

It not only strengthens our connection with God but it's also a powerful tool to overcome worry, doubt, fear, and the turmoil in our thoughts. We should pray about everything and be transparent with God. Our prayers should encompass praise, adoration, repentance, and confession. In doing so, we should acknowledge our shortcomings, seek cleansing, and make amends for past mistakes, even those rooted in our family history.

When we bring our needs and desires before God, we must ensure they align with His word and will.

Then, we must yield to His Holy Spirit, listen attentively to His response, and bask in His presence, for God speaks to us, and we must still hear His voice.

SCRIPTURES ON PRAYER (KJV)

1. **Thessalonians 5: 16-18**
   "Rejoice evermore. Pray without ceasing. In everything give thanks: for this is the will of God in Christ Jesus concerning you".
2. **Philippians 4: 6-7**
   "Be careful for nothing; but in every thing by prayer and supplication with thanksgiving let your request be made known unto God and the peace of God which passeth all understanding, shall keep your hearts

and minds through Christ Jesus".

3. **Jeremiah 33:3**
"Call unto me, and I will answer thee and shew thee great and mighty things, which thou knowest not".

4. **Matthew 6:6**
"But thou, when thou prayest, enter into thy closet, and when thou hast shut thy door, pray to thy Father which is in secret, and Thy Father which seeth in secret shall reward thee openly".

5. **James 5:16**
"Confess your faults one to another, and pray one for another, that ye may be healed. The effectual fervent prayer of the righteous man availeth much".

6. **Romans 8:26**
"Likewise the Spirit also helpeth our infirmities: for we know not what we should pray for as we ought: but the Spirit itself maketh intercession for us with groanings which cannot be uttered".

7. **John 10:27**
"My sheep hear my voice, and I know them, and they follow me".

PRAYER FOR PRAYER LIFE

Heavenly Father,

I thank You for the gift of prayer and the privilege to come before You openly and intimately. I lift the person reading this right now. Lord, draw them closer to You and deepen their desire to seek You in prayer. Remove every distraction, fear, and doubt that hinders them from fully embracing Your presence.

Teach them to pray boldly and humbly knowing You hear every word and care about every detail of their lives. Fill their hearts with a spirit of praise and adoration so that they may worship You in spirit and truth. Reveal any areas where repentance is needed and cleanse them from all unrighteousness.

They bring their needs and desires before You align their heart with Your will. Help them trust Your perfect timing and sovereign plan. Give them ears to hear Your voice clearly and the courage to obey Your leading. May their prayer life become a place of refuge, strength, and transformation. I pray for a fresh outpouring of Your Holy Spirit to guide them in every prayer and decision. Let them experience the joy and peace of being in communion with You. Strengthen their faith and remind them that You are always near.

In Yeshua's Name (Jesus), HalleluYah and it is so !

REFLECTION QUESTIONS ON PRAYER:

- How would you describe your current prayer life: consistent, occasional, or infrequent?
- Do you find it easy or challenging to be transparent with God? Why?
- What are some areas in your life where you need to trust God more through prayer?
- Do you intentionally include praise, repentance, and confession in your prayers?

JOURNALING:

FORGIVENESS

We often hear that forgiveness is a powerful gift we give ourselves. It frees us from the weight of resentment and bitterness that rob us of our well-being.

Forgiveness is not just for the other person; in most cases, it's for ourselves. We have all done things that require forgiveness. It's helpful to remember that we should all strive to be forgiving because we constantly need God's forgiveness. Without it, we are reminded of our imperfections.

We are reminded that holding onto grudges and unforgiveness can weigh heavily on our well-being, affect our health, and take up valuable space in our minds. Unforgiveness can hinder our spiritual growth, block blessings, and delay answers to our prayers. The scripture encourages us to forgive so that our heavenly Father can forgive us (Matthew 6:14-15).

Forgiveness involves willfully putting aside resentment toward someone who has wronged, been unfair or hurtful, or harmed us somehow. Forgiveness is not merely accepting what happened or ceasing to be angry; it is a powerful act of liberation where we voluntarily release feelings toward someone who has wronged us and rise above the associated pain.

By choosing forgiveness, one does not merely recognize the past or suppress feelings; instead, it takes profound steps toward healing and transformation.

Reference: (Matthew 18: 21-22) KJV.

(21 Then Peter came to him and said, Lord, how often shall my brother sin against me, and I forgive him? Till seven times?).

(22 Jesus saith unto him, I say not unto thee, until seven times: but, until seventy times seven).

The Holy Spirit empowers us to forgive as God commands, for forgiveness is a selfless, supernatural act that transcends human understanding. The

world may teach us to seek revenge and retaliate, but as followers of Christ, we are called to be set apart, embracing forgiveness as a reflection of God›s love. Remember, unforgiveness is a sin that can hinder our prayers (Psalm 66:18).

Choose to forgive, not in our strength, but through the power of the Holy Spirit.

In Yeshua's Name (Jesus), HalleluYah!! And it is so !

REFLECTION QUESTIONS:

• Who or what situation are you finding it hard to forgive and release today?

Start by writing it down. Write to release, cry out, pray, forgive, and become free and empowered to live more joyfully.

JOURNALING:

DEVOTIONAL: THE UNFAILING LOVE OF GOD (GOD'S LOVE)

"But God demonstrates His love toward us, in that while we were still sinners, Christ died for us."

— Romans 5:8

Lord, there was a time when I believed I had to earn Your love. If I prayed, fasted, worshipped, or fought hard enough in the spirit, I would be protected from pain. I poured out my heart in intercession for others, striving to be perfect, thinking it would make me more worthy of Your love. But even in my pursuit of holiness, I still experienced hurt, loss, and attacks that left me feeling abandoned. I questioned if You truly loved me.

And then, in my weakness, I fell. I let sin in. I drifted away. I had a prodigal season where I did not seek You as I once did. But even then—You never left me. Even when I walked away, You pursued me. Even when I fell short, You remained faithful. Your conviction never abandoned me. Your mercy covered me. Your love never wavered.

"If we are faithless, He remains faithful; He cannot deny Himself."

— 2 Timothy 2:13

PRAYER:

Lord, You have shown me that Your love is not something I have to earn—it is something You freely give. It was never about my perfection; it was always about Your grace. It was never about how much I could do for You; it was always about what You already did for me on the cross. Your love is unshakable. Even when I don't feel it, don't understand it, or miss the mark—You are still with me.

You have placed people in my path to remind me that I am seen and known. You have aligned my steps even when I didn't know where I was going. You have spoken to me in my lowest moments, reassuring me that I belong to You. And through it all, I have learned that Your love is more significant than my failures.

"Neither death nor life, neither angels nor demons, neither our fears for today nor our worries about tomorrow—not even the powers of hell can separate us from God's love."

— Romans 8:38

Father, I surrender the need to be perfect. I surrender the guilt of my past. I surrender the lie that I am only loved when I have it all together. I choose to rest in the truth that You love me entirely—not because of what I do, but because of who You are.

Thank You for keeping me, loving me, and never letting me go. I am Yours, and that is enough.

In Yeshua's Name (Jesus), HalleluYah and it is so !

REFLECTION QUESTIONS:

- Have you been trying to earn God's love instead of simply receiving it?
- How has God shown His love for you, even in seasons when you felt distant?
- In what ways can you rest in His grace instead of striving for perfection? You are loved. You are held. You are His. Always.

JOURNALING:

DAY 4

DEVOTIONAL: TRUSTING GOD IN THE WAITING

"Wait on the Lord; be of good courage, and He shall strengthen your heart; wait, I say, on the Lord!"

— Psalm 27:14

Lord, I have prayed, cried, fasted, and believed. I have poured my heart before You, pleading for restoration, healing, and breakthrough. I have seen others receive their answers, yet I am still waiting. I am waiting for my marriage to be restored, for the pain of loss to ease, for my family to be whole again, for my brother's freedom, and for the day when my tears are no longer a daily companion.

The waiting is hard, Lord. The silence feels heavy. There are moments when doubt creeps in, whispering that maybe You've forgotten me. But even in my unanswered prayers, I choose to trust. Even when I don't see movement, I know You are working. Even when my heart aches, I believe You are near.

"Before they call, I will answer; while they are still speaking, I will hear."

— Isaiah 65:24

You see the prayers I have prayed in secret. You know the desires of my heart. And even when I don't see immediate answers, I hold onto the promise that You are a God who hears. Your delays are not denials. Your silence is not abandonment. You are refining me in the waiting, strengthening my faith, drawing me closer to You.

PRAYER:

Lord, help me to trust Your timing, even when I don't understand it. Help me praise You in the waiting, knowing that You are working all things together for my good. Give me the strength to stand, the faith to believe, and the patience to endure.

"For the vision is yet for an appointed time; but at the end, it will speak, and it will not lie. Though it tarries, wait for it; because it will surely come, it will not tarry."

— Habakkuk 2:3

I may not know when or how You will answer, but I know You will. You are not a man who should lie. Your promises are yes and amen. So, I will keep praying, believing, and waiting because You are faithful.

In Yeshua's Name (Jesus), HalleluYah!! And it is so !

REFLECTION QUESTIONS:

- What prayers have you been waiting on God to answer?
- How can you trust God more in the waiting season? What has God already done in your life that proves His faithfulness?

JOURNALING:

DEVOTIONAL: MERCY

Mercy is a profound act of kindness and compassion that transforms lives and inspires growth. From the perspective of the one extending mercy, mercy becomes a powerful catalyst for growth, encouraging us to embody compassion and kindness towards those who may not deserve it. There are two primary forms of mercy: (1) the gracious withholding of judgment or punishment and (2) a profound attitude of compassion and pity for others in distress, especially when punishing or harming them is within one›s power.

In God's mercy, He shows leniency, withholding punishment from sinners even though they deserve it.

Mercy is holding back the bad that's on your path.

Grace is giving you what you need but does not deserve.

Mercy is judgment withheld.

Grace is the ability to do that which we wouldn't otherwise be able to do.

Grace is being loved without necessarily doing anything to deserve or earn it.

When mercy comes to mind, it does not give us what we deserve. It is forgiveness upon forgiveness. Grace allows the space to live how we have been told, commanded, led, and loved.

We see that Mercy is when God relents from what we deserve.

Scripture tells us, "*It is of* the LORD›S mercies that we are not consumed because his compassions fail not. *They are* new every morning: great *is* thy faithfulness. Lamentations 3:22-23

In Yeshua's Name (Jesus), HalleluYah and it is so !

REFLECTION QUESTIONS:

- How often The Most High God has shown mercy towards you?
- How many times have you extended mercy to others?

JOURNALING:

DEVOTIONAL: CASTING YOUR CARES AT HIS FEET

"Cast all your cares upon Him, for He cares for you."

— 1 Peter 5:7

There are seasons in life when the weight of pain feels unbearable. Grief, loss, heartbreak, and uncertainty can all pile up, making it seem impossible to keep going. Maybe you are a mother grieving a child, a wife praying for a broken marriage to be restored, a daughter mourning the loss of a parent, or a sibling longing for the freedom of a loved one. Maybe you carry the silent pressure of being the strong one, the person others look to for faith and encouragement—even when you feel you have nothing left to give.

It is easy to feel overwhelmed, abandoned, or even forgotten in those moments. But God gently reminds us that we were never meant to carry these burdens alone. He invites us to lay them at His feet, surrendering the weight too heavy to bear.

"Come to Me, all you who labor and are heavy laden, and I will give you rest."

— Matthew 11:28

God sees your silent tears. He knows the prayers you whisper in the middle of the night. He understands the weariness of waiting for answers, healing, and restoration. Even when it feels like nothing is changing, he works behind the scenes. His peace is not dependent on circumstances but on knowing He is in control.

There is beauty in surrender. When you cast your cares on God, you are not giving up—you are entrusting them to the only One who can indeed carry them. You are choosing to trust that He is making all things new, even in suffering and loss.

"And we know that all things work together for good to those who love God, to those who are called according to His purpose."

— Romans 8:28

So today, choose to release it all to Him—your grief, fears, loneliness, and exhaustion. Give Him your broken pieces, unanswered prayers, and hopes for the future. You don't have to carry it alone, because He is your refuge. He is your strength. He is your peace.

Keep trusting. Keep believing. Keep worshiping—not because everything is perfect, but because He is. And in that, you will find rest.

PRAYER:

Father, I lay my burdens before You. You see my heart, my pain, and my longing for restoration. Help me to trust You in the waiting. Strengthen me when I feel weak, and remind me that I am never alone. I cast my cares at Your feet, knowing You are faithful and working all things together for my good.

In Yeshua's Name (Jesus), HalleluYah and it is so !

REFLECTION QUESTIONS:

- What burdens are you holding onto that you need to surrender to God?
- How has God given you peace when you thought you wouldn't survive?
- How can you remind yourself daily that God is working all things together for your good?

No matter the burden, His hands are strong enough to carry it. Keep casting. Keep trusting. Keep standing.

JOURNALING:

PEACE DEVOTIONAL: THE PEACE OF GOD IN THE STORM

"And the peace of God, which surpasses all understanding, will guard your hearts and minds through Christ Jesus."

— Philippians 4:7

Lord, my heart has been shattered by loss. I have buried my son, said goodbye to my father, and endured the heartbreak of a broken relationship. Grief has knocked on my door more times than I can bear, and yet, somehow, I am still standing. I should have lost my mind, but Your peace has held me together. I should have been consumed by sorrow, but Your presence has kept me afloat.

Nothing looks like what I prayed for, but I still choose to worship. My heart aches, but I still prefer to trust. I do not understand why life has unfolded this way, but I believe You are still God. You›re still good. Even in tears, I lift my hands and say, *You are faithful.*

"The Lord is near to the brokenhearted and saves the crushed in spirit."

— Psalm 34:18

Father, I do not grieve as one without hope. Though I feel the weight of this suffering, I know You are near. You collect every tear, sit with me in sorrow, and whisper peace over my soul. When the enemy tells me I am alone, I remind my heart that You will never leave me. I stand on Your promises when my circumstances tell me there is no way forward.

I don't have all the answers, but I trust the One who does. I may not see restoration yet, but I know You are the God who redeems. I release my pain into Your hands. I release the need to understand. I release every broken piece of my heart, knowing that You can heal what is beyond my ability to fix.

"You will keep in perfect peace those whose minds are steadfast because they trust in You."

— Isaiah 26:3

PRAYER:

Lord, I don't just want to survive this season—I want to experience Your peace in the middle of it. Let my life be a testimony that You are enough, even in the most profound grief, even in the hardest losses. Even when everything around me is uncertain, I stand firm in the truth that You are unshakable.

So today, I choose peace, worship, and trust. My heart is hurting, but it is still beating. My faith is tested, but it is still standing. And because of You, I will make it through.

In Yeshua's Name (Jesus), HalleluYah and it is so !

REFLECTION QUESTIONS:

- How have you seen God's peace sustain you in my hardest moments?
- What areas of your life must you release into God's hands?
- How can you continue to worship and trust, even when you don't understand?

Hold on, beloved. Peace is not found in understanding everything but in trusting the One who holds everything.

JOURNALING:

LONG-SUFFERING! DEVOTIONAL: FAITH THROUGH LONG SUFFERING

"Weeping may endure for a night, but joy comes in the morning."
— Psalm 30:5

"But those who wait on the Lord shall renew their strength; they shall mount up with wings like eagles, they shall run and not be weary, they shall walk and not faint."
— Isaiah 40:31

"And not only that, but we also glory in tribulations, knowing that tribulation produces perseverance; and perseverance, character; and character, hope. Now hope does not disappoint, because the love of God has been poured out in our hearts by the Holy Spirit who was given to us."
— Romans 5:3-5

Lord, I come before You amid deep sorrow, carrying a heart that aches from loss, abandonment, and unanswered questions. The weight of suffering feels unbearable, yet I lift my hands in worship, even in pain. I do not understand why this road is so complex or why grief and heartbreak seem unrelenting, but I know You are near to the brokenhearted.

Your Word tells me that suffering is not the end of my story. Even as I walk through the valley of the shadow of death, You are with me. I may not see restoration yet, but I trust Your perfect timing. I may feel abandoned, but You have never forsaken me. My tears are counted, my cries heard, and my faith, though tested, remains in You.

PRAYER:

Father, teach me to trust when I do not understand. Give me the strength to stand when grief knocks me down. Help my heart to worship even when I am weary. You are working all things for my good, even in this storm.

I surrender my pain, loss, and suffering into Your hands. I choose faith over fear, worship over despair, and trust over doubt. I know You are the God who heals, restores and redeems. My story is not over. My suffering is not wasted. You are still writing beauty from these ashes.

Lord, help me endure, to hope again, and to believe in Your promises. Even through the tears, I will say: You are good, faithful, and with me.

In Yeshua's Name (Jesus), HalleluYah and it is so !

REFLECTION:

- How do you define long-suffering in your own words?
- What has your current or past long-suffering season taught you about yourself and your faith?
- Do you believe God has a purpose in your suffering? Why or Why Not?
- In what ways has long suffering stretched or strengthened your faith?

JOURNALING:

THANKSGIVING DEVOTIONAL: A HEART OF THANKSGIVING IN EVERY SEASON

"Give thanks in all circumstances, for this is the will of God in Christ Jesus for you."

— 1 Thessalonians 5:18

It's easy to be thankful when things are going well—when life feels smooth, worries are few, and relationships are easy. But what about when life feels heavy? When the world around you seems to be falling apart, when you're dealing with loss, or when the pain seems overwhelming? Can we still find reasons to be thankful in those moments?

I've been there—when grief weighed so heavily on my heart that simply getting through the day felt like a struggle, when unanswered prayers left me wondering if God was still listening. But even in those moments, God has shown me that thanksgiving is not just about celebrating the good times—it's about acknowledging that He is still present, faithful, and good, even when nothing looks the way we expect.

"I will bless the Lord at all times; His praise shall continually be in my mouth."

Psalm 34:1

Thanksgiving is an act of remembering. It focuses on God's goodness, even when life doesn't go as planned. When everything seems uncertain, it can be a grounding reminder to reflect on what remains constant: God's love, presence, and promises.

In my own life, I've learned that giving thanks in hard times doesn't deny the pain—it acknowledges that God's goodness is still at work, even when I can't see the complete picture. There have been days when I simply thanked God for the strength to get out of bed, for the breath in my lungs, and small moments of peace in the chaos. I've felt His presence most clearly in these simple, raw moments.

"Oh, give thanks to the Lord, for He is good, for His steadfast love endures forever!"

— 1 Chronicles 16:34

Thanksgiving doesn't mean everything has to be perfect. It's about shifting our focus, even if just for a moment, from our circumstances to the truth that God's love never fails. It's remembering that we can be thankful because, no matter where we are, He's with us—helping us through the hard days, comforting us in our pain, and walking with us every step of the way.

So today, take a moment to reflect. What are you thankful for, even in the midst of difficulty? It may not be easy, but giving thanks for the small or the big things reminds us that God is still working, moving, and faithful. That way, we can find peace, hope, and strength to keep going.

PRAYER:

Father, even in the most challenging seasons, I give thanks. Thank You for Your unwavering presence, constant love, and goodness, especially when things are difficult. Help me remember that I am never alone and trust that You are working all things together for my good.

In Yeshua's Name (Jesus), HalleluYah and it is so !

REFLECTION QUESTIONS:

- What small things can you give thanks for today, even if things feel hard?
- How has God shown His faithfulness in challenging periods?

JOURNALING:

HOLINESS: DEVOTIONAL: THE CALL TO HOLINESS IN TODAY'S WORLD

"But as He who called you is holy, you also be holy in all your conduct, because it is written, 'Be holy, for I am holy.'"
— 1 Peter 1:15-16

In today's world, it can feel like the idea of holiness has become an outdated concept, something that doesn't quite fit with the hustle and bustle of modern life. We're bombarded with messages encouraging us to follow our desires, indulge in what feels good, and live for ourselves. But as believers, we are called to something different—a life set apart, a life of holiness.

Holiness isn't about perfection; it's about living in a way that reflects God's character. It's about living according to His standards, not the world's. It's about walking in integrity, purity, and continually striving to be more like Christ. In a world that promotes self-centeredness, holiness calls us to be God-centered. It's not just about avoiding sin; it's about pursuing God with our whole heart, mind, and life.

"Therefore, since we have these promises, beloved, let us cleanse ourselves from every defilement of body and spirit, bringing holiness to completion in the fear of God."
— 2 Corinthians 7:1

Holiness is not about following a list of do's and don'ts. It's about aligning our lives with God's will, recognizing that we are created in His image, and choosing to live in a way that honors that truth. In a culture that often celebrates compromise, the call to holiness requires us to stand firm in our faith and be a light in the darkness. It may not always be easy, but the pursuit of holiness is always worth it.

In my journey, I've learned that holiness doesn't come without its challenges. There have been moments when I felt crushed by grief, moments when I wanted to retreat into anger and bitterness, and moments when my heart wanted to wallow in pain. Losing my son, facing a broken marriage, and enduring seasons of abandonment and isolation—it all felt like a deep test of my faith and my commitment to holiness. How could I remain holy when life was falling apart around me? How could I stand firm when my heart was breaking?

During such times, I doubted myself and questioned if God was even working in my life. But through every season of hardship, I've learned that holiness isn't about being free from struggle—it's about how we respond to those struggles. My challenges didn't pull me away from holiness; they pushed me deeper into it. I trusted God when I could have chosen anger or despair. When I could have chosen bitterness, I chose forgiveness. When I could have chosen to close my heart to others, I decided to love.

Even when I didn't feel His presence and couldn't see the answers to my prayers, I chose to honor God. I've come to realize that holiness is an act of surrender. It's choosing God above all else, especially when everything around you crumbles. The path to holiness may not always be smooth, but it always leads to peace, purpose, and restoration.

"Strive for peace with everyone, and for the holiness without which no one will see the Lord."

— Hebrews 12:14

Holiness is the foundation of our witness to the world. Our lives are meant to point others to Christ; how we live is a testimony of the God we serve. In a world filled with uncertainty, pain, and brokenness, holiness is a beacon of hope. It shows others that there is a better way—a way of peace, purity, and purpose.

Living a life of holiness doesn't mean we won't face struggles. It often means we'll face challenges and opposition. But the beauty of holiness is that it isn't about what we can do on our own—it's about the power of the Holy Spirit working in and through us. Holiness is not something we can achieve on our own; it's a work of grace.

Today, take a moment to reflect on your life. Are there areas where you're compromising? Are there areas where you're allowing the world's standards to define you instead of God's? Remember, holiness is not about being perfect but being set apart. God is calling you to be different—not so you can stand out, but so you can reflect His glory in the world around you.

PRAYER:

Father, I come before You today with a desire to live a life of holiness. I know that I cannot achieve this without You, but with Your Spirit, I can. Help me align my heart with Your will to live in a way that reflects Your love and character. Help me to stand firm in my faith, to resist the pull of the world, and to be a light to those around me. I want my life to bring You glory.

In Yeshua's Name (Jesus), HalleluYah and it is so !

REFLECTION QUESTIONS:

- How do you define holiness in your own life?
- What does it mean for you to be "set apart" for God?
- How can you pursue holiness in both your thoughts and actions daily?
- Can you identify when your decision to pursue holiness led to greater peace or healing?

JOURNALING:

DAY 11

DEVOTIONAL: FAITH ON THE JOURNEY

"For we walk by faith, not by sight."

— 2 Corinthians 5:7

Life often feels like a journey full of unexpected twists and turns. We face moments of deep joy and crushing grief, times of success and failure, and seasons of peace and struggle. In my own life, I've walked through the most difficult of paths—losing my youngest son, enduring a broken marriage, navigating family loss, and even facing loneliness and isolation in moments when I most needed connection. These trials have been painful, often leaving me wondering if I could go on. But in every moment, I've learned that faith is the key to persevering.

Faith is not just about believing when everything is going well. It's about trusting God when life is hard, when nothing seems to make sense, and when the weight of grief and hardship feels like it will crush you. It's easy to have faith when things are going according to plan, but the true test of faith comes when the plan doesn't seem to make sense, and the road ahead is unclear.

In my life, I've often found myself at a crossroads where the path ahead was shrouded in darkness, where the only thing I could hold onto was God's promise that He would never leave me. Losing my son was one of the hardest trials I've ever faced. In those early days of grief, I couldn't see how I could ever move forward. The pain was overwhelming. Yet, in the middle of my grief, I heard God whisper: *"Walk with Me. Trust Me."*

Even in pain, I knew my faith in God could not be shaken. My journey wasn't about having all the answers but knowing that God was with me in every moment, whether I could feel Him or not. Faith is all about this: it's choosing to trust God even when you don't have all the answers. It's believing He's working in ways you can't see and knowing He has a purpose for every season of life, even the painful ones.

"Now faith is the assurance of things hoped for, the conviction of things not seen."

— Hebrews 11:1

I've had to live this out daily. There have been days when I didn't feel like praying, when I wanted to give up, and when the weight of my responsibilities as a mother, wife, and woman of faith felt unbearable. But I've learned that faith is not a feeling—it's a choice. Getting up is a choice, even when I don't feel like it. It's a choice to trust God even when life feels uncertain. And in making that choice, I've experienced a deeper strength than I ever could have imagined.

Faith doesn't mean that everything will go as planned or that our pain will instantly disappear. But it means we don't have to face our journey alone. God is with us every step of the way, holding us up when we are too weak to stand, comforting us when we are broken, and giving us hope even in the darkest times.

"For I know the plans I have for you, declares the Lord, plans for welfare and not for evil, to give you a future and a hope."
— Jeremiah 29:11

Even when the road is tough, we can be assured that God has a purpose for our lives and is working all things together for our good (Romans 8:28). The key is to keep moving forward, even when we don't understand the journey. Faith gives us the courage to keep walking, trusting, and believing in the midst of hardship.

I know the path isn't always easy. There are moments where you may want to quit, where you question if your faith is enough. But remember: faith is not about having all the answers, but about trusting in the One who does. It's about knowing that even when we can't see the end of the road, God leads us to something greater than we can imagine.

PRAYER:

Father, I thank You for the faith that You have placed in my heart. Even during trials, I choose to trust You. My journey is not always easy, but I also know that You are with me every step of the way. Help me walk by faith, not sight, trusting that You are working all things for my good. Strengthen my heart and spirit as I continue this journey, and remind me that I am never alone.

In Yeshua's Name (Jesus), HalleluYah and it is so !

REFLECTION QUESTIONS:

- What areas of your life are you struggling to trust God with?
- How can you cultivate a deeper faith in God, especially during times of uncertainty?
- What is one way you can actively walk by faith today, even if you don't have all the answers?

Even in the hardest moments, keep walking by faith. God is with you and faithful to complete the good work He has started in your life.

JOURNALING:

DEVOTIONAL: SPIRITUAL WARFARE – FIGHTING WITH FAITH AND FERVENT PRAYER

"For we do not wrestle against flesh and blood, but against the rulers, against the authorities, against the cosmic powers over this present darkness, against the spiritual forces of evil in the heavenly places."
— Ephesians 6:12

Over the years, I've come to understand the reality of spiritual warfare deeply. Life often feels like a series of battles, with attacks that don't just come from people or situations but from an unseen enemy who seeks to destroy everything God is doing in our lives. Whether we realize it or not, we're in a spiritual battle every day. The enemy works tirelessly to attack our faith, our peace, and our connection with God, especially in moments of loss, grief, or personal struggle.

For me, the battles have been relentless. After losing my youngest son, enduring marriage struggles, and facing the deaths of close family members, the enemy tried to steal my joy, my faith, and my trust in God's goodness. I've felt the weight of his attacks on my heart, my mind, and even my body. There were moments when the enemy tried to convince me that God had forgotten me, that my prayers were powerless, and that I would never overcome my pain. But through it all, I've learned that the key to overcoming these attacks is fervent prayer, faith, and the armor of God.

FERVENT PRAYER: A POWERFUL WEAPON

In the face of these attacks, fervent prayer has been my weapon of choice. When I felt overwhelmed and couldn't find the strength to continue, I turned to prayer. It wasn't always easy to pray when I felt so broken, but I knew prayer was my lifeline. Fervent prayer is not just about asking for things—it's about crying out to God from the depths of our hearts, trusting that He hears us even when we don't have the words. It's a way to push back the enemy's lies, to find strength when we're weak, and to invite God's presence into our lives.

I've prayed in the middle of my grief, in the quiet of the night, and during moments of doubt. And I've seen God show up in powerful ways. He has strengthened my faith, restored my peace, and reminded me that He is greater than any battle I face. Prayer is not passive; it's an active declaration of faith, reminding the enemy that God is in control.

"The effective, fervent prayer of a righteous man avails much."

— James 5:16

HOW THE ENEMY WILL ATTACK YOUR FAITH

The enemy uses many tactics to try and weaken your faith. These are some of the ways I've seen the enemy attack and how I've had to stand firm in prayer and faith to overcome them:

1. **Doubt and Unbelief**: While facing hard seasons, the enemy tries to plant seeds of doubt in our hearts. He whispers, "God isn't listening," or "He doesn't care." In those moments, I've had to remind myself of God's promises and speak truth over my life. Prayer helps me silence the doubts and declare God's faithfulness.

2. **Isolation and Loneliness**: The enemy often makes us feel alone, especially in our struggles. He wants us to believe that we're the only ones going through hardship and that no one understands. But I've learned that God is with me even in moments of isolation. My prayers keep me connected to Him; when I feel alone, I call on the Holy Spirit to fill the gaps.

3. **Fear and Anxiety**: Fear can easily take root in our hearts, especially when facing the unknown. The enemy wants us to be consumed with anxiety and worry, but I've had to choose faith over fear continually. Prayer has been a way for me to release my worries to God, knowing that He holds my future.

4. **Bitterness and Unforgiveness**: When we are hurt by others, the enemy tries to plant bitterness in our hearts. He deceives us into thinking that

holding onto unforgiveness will give us control. But I've had to choose to forgive, not for others but for my freedom. Prayer has been the key to healing my heart and letting go of the weight of bitterness.

5. **Discouragement**: The enemy wants to wear us down, to make us feel like giving up is the only option. I've been there—feeling like I couldn't go on any longer. But I've learned that in those moments, I have to press into prayer and remind myself of the truth that God is still working, even when I can't see it.

6. **The Lies of the Enemy**: One of the most significant attacks on our faith is the enemy's lies. He'll tell us we're unworthy, that we've messed up too badly, or that God will never forgive us. I've struggled with these lies myself, but over time I've learned to recognize them as the enemy's tactics. In prayer, I rise against those lies, speaking the truth of God's Word over my life.

PUTTING ON THE FULL ARMOR OF GOD

In such moments of battle, I've learned the importance of putting on the full armor of God. Ephesians 6:10-18 tells us to stand firm, equipped with the belt of truth, the breastplate of righteousness, the shoes of peace, the shield of faith, the helmet of salvation, and the sword of the Spirit. This armor is essential for facing the enemy's attacks. It's a reminder that we're not fighting in our strength but in God's power.

When I face spiritual battles, I remind myself of God's Word—His promises, truth, and protection. I pray confidently, knowing that no attack from the enemy is stronger than God's power. And I stand firm in the knowledge that in Christ, I am more than a conqueror (Romans 8:37).

PRAYER:

Father, I thank You for equipping me with everything I need to fight the enemy. I know that my battle is not against flesh and blood but against the forces of darkness. Help me stand firm in Your truth, put on God's full armor, and fight with fervent prayer. I resist the enemy's lies and declare that my faith will not be shaken. Strengthen me when I am weak, and remind me that You are always with me. I trust in Your power to overcome every attack.

In Yeshua›s Name (Jesus), HalleluYah and it is so !

REFLECTION QUESTIONS:

- How has the enemy attacked your faith recently?
- What areas of your life do you need to stand firm in faith and resist the enemy?
- How can you use fervent prayer as a weapon in your spiritual battles?

Remember, the enemy always seeks to attack, but we have been equipped to overcome. Stand firm in prayer, put on the full armor of God, and trust that He is with you every step of the way.

JOURNALING:

DAY 13

DEVOTIONAL: OVERCOMING FEAR WITH FAITH

"For God has not given us a spirit of fear, but of power and of love and of a sound mind."

— 2 Timothy 1:7

Fear is something we all face, whether it's the fear of the unknown, fear of loss, or fear of not being good enough. For me, fear has shown up in many forms—fear of losing my family, fear of not being able to overcome the challenges I've faced, fear of walking through seasons of grief and loss. It's something that feels heavy, even paralyzing at times. But through my journey, I've learned that fear doesn't have to define or control me.

I've experienced loss—losing my son, losing my dad, and enduring a broken marriage—and each of these experiences could have easily led me to give in to fear. Fear of not being able to stand, fear of being crushed by my circumstances, and fear of being alone in my pain. But I've come to understand that fear is not from God, and it doesn't have the final say.

FEAR IS REAL, BUT GOD'S POWER IS GREATER

Fear is real, and we all experience it in our human journey. But the truth is that fear doesn't have to be our identity. It doesn't define who we are or where we're going. I've learned that while fear can show up in my heart and mind, I don't have to let it control my actions or future.

There have been moments when fear felt suffocating—like when I was facing uncertainty in my marriage, grieving the loss of my son, or feeling isolated from loved ones. In those moments, fear whispered that I wouldn't make it through. But instead of allowing it to dominate my thoughts, I chose to turn to God's Word and prayer. His promises remind me that He is with me in my weakness, and His strength will carry me.

"The Lord is my light and my salvation; whom shall I fear? The Lord is the stronghold of my life; of whom shall I be afraid?"

— Psalm 27:1

THE LIE OF FEAR

One of the biggest lies fear tries to tell us is that we are alone. It tries to convince us that we will never get through our struggles and that the grief, the loss, and the pain will always define us. But in moments of fear, I've learned to cry out to God, acknowledging that I am weak, but He is strong. When the enemy tries to use fear to paralyze me, I remind myself of God's truth: He is with me, and He is for me.

Fear can make us believe we are unworthy of God's love or that our pain is too much for Him to handle, but we must reject those lies. Our fear does not define us. We are defined by God's love, His peace, and His power at work within us.

"So we can confidently say, 'The Lord is my helper; I will not fear; what can man do to me?'"

— Hebrews 13:6

REPLACING FEAR WITH FAITH

Faith is the antidote to fear. I've learned that in the face of fear, the best thing I can do is remind myself of God's promises and His faithfulness. Fear tells me what might go wrong, but faith reminds me of what God can do. In my darkest moments, when everything around me felt uncertain, I had to choose faith over fear.

I've seen firsthand that God meets me in my fears. Whether I'm facing grief, loneliness, or fear of failure, God's peace is stronger than any fear I face. Praying and speaking His Word over my life brings peace that surpasses understanding. It's not always easy, but every time I step out in faith, I see God move in ways that encourage my heart and strengthen my spirit.

"Do not fear, for I have redeemed you; I have called you by name, you are mine."

— Isaiah 43:1

PRACTICAL STEPS TO OVERCOME FEAR

1. **Acknowledge the Fear**: Don't deny that fear exists, but don't let it control you either. Acknowledge it and face it, then give it to God in prayer.
2. **Speak God's Word**: When fear tries to grip your heart, speak the truth of God's Word. Declare that you are not alone, that He will never leave or forsake you (Hebrews 13:5).
3. **Remember His Promises**: In moments of fear, remind yourself of God's faithfulness. Reflect on times when He has carried you through.
4. **Worship**: Fear cannot thrive in a heart that worships God. In your fear, lift your voice and trust that He is bigger than what you face.
5. **Surround Yourself with Faith**: Surround yourself with people who encourage you in your faith. Community is key when facing fear and uncertainty.

PRAYER:

Lord, I come before You today acknowledging the fear that sometimes tries to take root in my heart. Whether it's fear of loss, fear of failure, or fear of what lies ahead, I know that You are more significant than any fear I face. Help me trust in Your love and power, knowing that You have not given me a spirit of fear but of power, love, and a sound mind. I choose faith today, Lord, and I ask that You replace every fear with Your peace. Strengthen my heart, guide me in Your truth, and remind me that I am never alone.

In Yeshua's Name (Jesus), HalleluYah and it is so !

REFLECTION QUESTIONS:

- What fears are you facing now that you must surrender to God?
- How can you replace fear with faith today?

- In what ways has God proven His faithfulness to you in the past?

Remember, fear may show up, but it does not define you. God's power, love, and peace will always be greater than anything fear can bring. Trust in His truth, and let His perfect love cast out all fear.

JOURNALING:

DEVOTIONAL ON HOPE

"For I know the plans I have for you," declares the Lord, "plans to prosper you and not to harm you, plans to give you a hope and a future."

— Jeremiah 29:11

Hope. We all need it, especially when life doesn't make sense. When everything around us seems to be falling apart—the loss of a loved one, a broken relationship, or a season of struggle—hope can feel like the last thing we have. In those moments of despair, imagining hope on the horizon can feel nearly impossible.

But in those moments of difficulty, we must remember that hope is not just a fleeting feeling—it's a choice. It's a decision to trust that God is still good, even when life doesn't go as expected. When we face trials and hardships, hope isn't found in our present circumstances; it's found in the truth that God has a plan, even in our pain.

HOPE IS ANCHORED IN GOD'S PROMISES

When we face trials, it can seem like there is no way out. But even in our darkest hours, God's promises anchor us. The Bible is full of reminders that God sees us, He hears us, and He has a plan that we can trust. Even when we can't see the way forward, we can rest in the hope that He is always working behind the scenes, even when we don't understand what's happening.

Romans 5:3-5 *says, "Not only so, but we also glory in our sufferings because we know that suffering produces perseverance; perseverance, character; and character, hope. And hope does not put us to shame because God's love has been poured out into our hearts through the Holy Spirit, who has been given to us."*

Hope is often refined through suffering. It's in the struggles that we learn to persevere and build character. We may not see it now, but God is using the challenges we face to shape, grow, and strengthen our hope. He's teaching us to trust Him, even when it's hard because we know His plans are for our good.

HOPE REQUIRES TRUST, EVEN WHEN YOU DON'T UNDERSTAND

One of the hardest parts of holding onto hope is trusting when we don't understand why things are happening the way they are. There are so many times when life is confusing and painful, and we can't make sense of what's unfolding. But even in those moments, we must trust that God is still good, that He hasn't abandoned us, and that He has a purpose for every moment of pain.

> **Proverbs 3:5 - 6** *says, "Trust in the Lord with all your heart and lean not on your own understanding; in all your ways submit to Him, and He will make your paths straight."*

We don't always have the answers; sometimes, we still don't understand why things unfold the way they do. But we can trust God, even in the unknown. He sees the bigger picture, and His timing is perfect. Hope doesn't mean having all the answers; it means trusting that God has a bigger and better plan than anything we can see right now.

MAINTAINING HOPE: A DAILY CHOICE

Maintaining hope isn't always easy. Some days, it feels like the weight of life is too heavy to bear, and the path ahead seems unclear. But hope is a choice we must make daily. Even when we don't feel like it, we can choose to hope because we know God is faithful.

One way to maintain hope is to fill our hearts and minds with God's Word. The Bible is full of reminders of God's goodness, faithfulness, and promises. When we feel discouraged, we can turn to Scripture and remind ourselves of our hope in Christ. Meditating on verses that encourage our hearts and lift our eyes toward God can help us maintain hope, no matter our circumstances.

Isaiah 40:31 *says, "But those who hope in the Lord will renew their strength. They will soar on wings like eagles; they will run and not grow weary; they will walk and not be faint."*

When we place our hope in the Lord, He renews our strength. He gives us the power to keep going, even when we can't take another step. He promises to provide us with the endurance we need to press on, no matter how hard the journey.

PRAYER:

Lord, I come before You today with a heart that sometimes struggles to hold on to hope. Life can be overwhelming, and the weight of my pain feels heavy. But I choose to trust in Your promises. I hold onto the hope that You are with me, have a plan for my life, and are working on everything together for my good. Even when I don't understand, I will continue to trust in Your faithfulness. Renew my strength, Lord. Help me to hope in You, no matter what my circumstances look like.

In Yeshua's Name (Jesus), HalleluYah and it is so !

REFLECTION QUESTIONS:

- What areas of your life do you need to choose hope in today?
- How has God shown His faithfulness to you in difficult seasons?
- What Scripture can you turn to when you need to be reminded of your hope in Christ?

Hope is a choice. It's believing God is working, even when we can't see it. Keep choosing hope because, with God, your future is filled with promise.

JOURNALING:

THE POWER OF PRAISE IN TRIALS

"I will bless the Lord at all times; His praise shall continually be in my mouth."

— Psalm 34:1

Praise is one of the most powerful weapons a believer can wield, yet it's often one of the most difficult to access during trials. When life feels overwhelming, our hearts are heavy, and when we're faced with pain, the natural response may be to retreat, hold back, or question why we're going through such hardship. But in those moments, praise becomes even more critical.

Praise is not only an act of worship, but it's also a declaration of faith. It's acknowledging the greatness of God even when circumstances tell us otherwise. When we lift our voices in praise, we are reaffirming that God is still in control, that He is worthy of our worship, and that His goodness never changes, no matter what we're facing.

PRAISE IS A CHOICE, NOT JUST A FEELING

There are days when praise feels easy. The sun is shining, life feels good, and we're grateful. But there are other days when the weight of our struggles makes it difficult to even think about lifting our hands in worship. On those days, praise is a choice. It's choosing to worship despite what we see or feel, choosing to acknowledge that God is worthy regardless of our circumstances.

Hebrews 13:15 *says, "Through Jesus, therefore, let us continually offer to God a sacrifice of praise—the fruit of lips that openly profess his name."*

Praise is called a "sacrifice" because it often costs us something. It costs us our pride, our doubt, and our worry. It requires us to lay aside our hopelessness and declare that God remains faithful. But when we choose to praise, we invite God into our situations, and He begins to move in ways we can't always anticipate.

PRAISE SHIFTS OUR FOCUS

When life is hard, focusing solely on our problems is easy. The weight of trials can block our view of God's goodness, and we can find ourselves consumed by anxiety, worry, and fear. But when we praise, we shift our focus from the storm to the One who calms it.

In **Acts 16:25-26**, we see a powerful example of how praise shifts our perspective. Paul and Silas were imprisoned for preaching the gospel. They were beaten, bound, and left in a dark, cold dungeon. Yet, in the middle of their pain, they chose to praise. *"Paul and Silas were praying and singing hymns to God about midnight, and the other prisoners listened. Suddenly, the prison's foundations were shaken by such a violent earthquake. All the prison doors flew open at once, and everyone's chains came loose."*

Their praise not only brought freedom to them but also impacted the others around them. When we praise God in the midst of our struggles, we open ourselves up to His power and His presence. Praise shifts our perspective and reminds us that God is still sovereign and faithful at work, even when we don't see immediate results.

PRAISE IS AN ACT OF FAITH

Praise in the midst of hardship is a powerful act of faith .In times of trials—doubts ,questions ,or discouragement can easily take hold ,but choosing to praise in those moments declares our trust in Him ,even when we don't understand the reasons behind our circumstances .It's saying" ,I may not have all the answers ,but I trust You ,God .I believe You are still good ,and I will praise You through this storm".

Psalm 42:5 *says, "Why, my soul, are you downcast? Why so disturbed within me? Put your hope in God, for I will yet praise Him, my Savior and my God."*

David wrote these words in a time of deep despair. He was struggling but reminded himself to put his hope in God and continue praising, for God is worthy no matter the circumstances.

PRAISE BRINGS BREAKTHROUGH

When we are in the middle of a trial, we often feel powerless. But praise gives us access to a power far beyond our own. When we praise, we invite God to move in ways we can't see or imagine. He inhabits the praises of His people, and in His presence, there is freedom, peace, and breakthrough.

In **2 Chronicles 20:22**, King Jehoshaphat faced a massive enemy army. Instead of relying on his military strength, he sent the choir out first to praise God. *"As they began to sing and praise, the Lord set ambushes against the men of Ammon and Moab and Mount Seir who were invading Judah, and they were defeated."*

God fought for His people in response to their praise. When we praise in the middle of our trials, we invite God to fight on our behalf. Praise doesn't just change our hearts—it invites God's supernatural intervention.

PRAYER:

Lord, thank You for the power of praise. Even in the midst of my struggles, I choose to worship You. I may not understand why I'm going through this trial, but I trust that You are still in control. I declare Your goodness, faithfulness, and sovereignty over my life. I praise You because You are worthy, and I believe You will work all things for my good. Strengthen my faith as I worship, and let my praise be a weapon that brings breakthrough.

In Yeshua's Name (Jesus), HalleluYah and it is so !

REFLECTION QUESTIONS:

- How can you choose to praise God even when life is difficult?
- When was the last time you experienced a shift in your perspective through praise?

- What breakthrough do you believe God can bring through your praise today?

Praise is a weapon, a choice, and an act of faith. In the trials and tribulations of life, let your praise rise and watch God move in mighty ways.

JOURNALING:

WORSHIP – MORE THAN PRAISE, A RELATIONSHIP

"Yet a time is coming and has now come when the true worshipers will worship the Father in the Spirit and in truth, for they are the kind of worshipers the Father seeks."

—John 4:23

Worshiping is a deeply intimate experience. It is not merely an expression of gratitude for what God has done, but a moment where we commune with Him, express our love for Him, and draw closer to His heart. While praise is powerful in declaring God's greatness and His goodness, worship is more relational—it goes deeper, connecting us with God in the quiet places of our hearts.

WORSHIP: AN INTIMATE ENCOUNTER WITH GOD

When life feels heavy, when the pain seems unbearable, and when hope is hard to find, worshiping has a way of drawing us close to God›s heart. Worship is more than the songs we sing or the words we speak. It's an overflow of our hearts, a surrender to God's will, and a deep longing to connect with Him personally. It's the language of the heart, where we are vulnerable and authentic with our Creator.

In my own life, worship has been my refuge. Through the heartache, the losses, and the trials, worship has allowed me to express my deepest pain and surrender it to God. In worship, I can be raw, honest, and real. Worship has been where my tears have flowed, but I've also felt His peace, presence, and love in ways words cannot fully describe. Worship has been my anchor, lifeline, and source of strength.

WORSHIP VS. PRAISE: A DEEPER CONNECTION

While praise is powerful in its own right, worship is about building a deeper connection with God. Praise acknowledges God's greatness, but worship goes further—it connects our spirit to His. Praise can be loud, energetic, and celebratory, while worship often carries a quiet reverence, a humility, and a focus on God's presence rather than His actions.

> *In **Psalm 95:6**, it says, "Come, let us bow down in worship, let us kneel before the Lord our Maker." This is an invitation to worship with humility and reverence. When we worship, we bow our hearts before God, acknowledging He is our Creator, Sustainer, and Redeemer. It's a moment of surrender, where we recognize His worthiness and allow His presence to fill the spaces in our hearts.*

WORSHIP IN THE MIDST OF TRIALS

It's easy to praise God when everything is going well, but worship during difficult times shows our trust in God, even when the circumstances don't make sense. In moments of pain and loss, worship becomes a declaration that we are still choosing to be with God, even when life feels overwhelming.

> *In **Habakkuk 3:17-18**, the prophet writes, "Though the fig tree does not bud and there are no grapes on the vines, though the olive crop fails and the fields produce no food, though there are no sheep in the pen and no cattle in the stalls, yet I will rejoice in the Lord, I will be joyful in God my Savior." Even when everything around us seems to be falling apart, worship lets us declare that our joy and hope are in God alone.*

I have learned that worship is not just a response to God's blessings but a choice to remain in His presence. It's a choice to focus on His goodness even when our circumstances tell us otherwise. Worship becomes our weapon against despair and discouragement, allowing us to declare God's truth over the lies that our pain tells us.

WORSHIP AS A LIFESTYLE

Worship isn't just a Sunday activity or a moment of singing. It's a lifestyle, a constant awareness of God's presence. It's in the quiet moments when we choose to thank God, when we choose to seek His face, and when we choose to surrender our desires to His will. Worship is found in the everyday moments of life—washing dishes, driving to work, or sitting in quiet reflection.

Romans 12:1 *reminds us of this truth: "Therefore, I urge you, brothers and sisters, because of God's mercy, to offer your bodies as a living sacrifice, holy and pleasing to God—this is your true and proper worship." True worship goes beyond music; it's about offering our lives to God in gratitude for His mercy and grace. It's an ongoing conversation with Him, where we seek His presence in everything we do.*

WORSHIP BRINGS HEALING AND STRENGTH

Worship has the power to heal and restore. It invites God's presence to dwell in our hearts, and in His presence, there is peace. In worship, we can surrender our fears, anxieties, and burdens to God. When I find myself struggling, when the world›s weight feels too heavy, I turn to worship. I allow the music, the words, and the stillness to lead me into God's presence, where I can lay down my fears and be filled with His peace.

Psalm 147:3 *says, "He heals the brokenhearted and binds up their wounds."*

Worship has a way of ministering to our hearts and healing places we didn't even know were broken. In the quiet moments of worship, I have found God's healing touch, His comfort, and His love.

PRAYER:

Lord, thank You for the gift of worship. Thank You that we can come near to Your heart in worship and find peace, healing, and strength. Help me to worship You not just with my words but with my life. Teach me to seek You in the midst of my trials, to find joy in Your presence, and to offer my heart in surrender. I choose to worship You in spirit and truth, trusting that You are with me in every moment.

In Yeshua's Name (Jesus), HalleluYah and it is so !

REFLECTION QUESTIONS:

- How can you cultivate a lifestyle of worship in your everyday life?
- What areas of your life do you need to surrender to God in worship?
- How has worship brought healing to your heart in the past?

Worship is more than a song; it's a relationship with the One who created us. In times of joy and sorrow, worship draws us close to His heart, where we find the peace, strength, and healing we need to endure.

JOURNALING:

OBEDIENCE – HEARING GOD'S VOICE AND TRUSTING HIS WILL

"But Samuel replied, 'Does the Lord delight in burnt offerings and sacrifices as much as in obeying the Lord? To obey is better than sacrifice, and to heed is better than the fat of rams.'"

— 1 Samuel 15:22

Obedience to God is not always easy, but it is always worth it. It's the pathway to God's blessings, peace, and purpose for our lives. We believers are called to hear God's voice and respond to His leading, even when the road seems uncertain or complex. Obedience is not just a set of actions; it's a posture of the heart—trusting that God knows what's best and following His direction even when we don't understand the complete picture.

THE CHALLENGE OF RADICAL OBEDIENCE

One of the hardest steps in my journey of faith was when I felt God leading me to leave everything behind—my home, my support system, and everything familiar—to move to a place where I had no family. I had my children with me but no one else to rely on. I had no idea what the future would look like or how I would manage, but I knew God had called me. And though it was difficult and scary, I chose to step out in obedience.

There were days when I doubted my decision, days when I questioned if I heard God right, and days when the loneliness and uncertainty felt overwhelming. But in those moments, God's presence reminded me that His plans for me are always good, even when they require radical obedience. The more I walked in faith, the more I saw the blessings unfold. God opened doors, provided in unexpected ways, and deepened my trust in Him with every step.

OBEDIENCE AS THE KEY TO GOD'S WILL

Obedience is essential to understanding God's will for our lives. It's through our willingness to obey, even when it's difficult or uncomfortable, that we experience God's guidance and blessing. When we obey, we show God that we trust Him, and He responds by revealing more of His plan for us.

Romans 12:2 encourages us to be transformed by renewing our minds so that we may know God's will—His good, pleasing, and perfect will. But this transformation comes through obedience. When we step out in faith and follow His voice, we align ourselves with His purpose, and His will becomes clearer.

Obedience also strengthens our relationship with God. Just as any relationship deepens through trust and communication, our connection with God grows when we hear His voice and obey His commands. Obedience draws us closer to Him and helps us grow in our faith and dependence on Him.

LISTENING TO GOD'S VOICE

The key to obedience is hearing God's voice. But how do we hear His voice in the noise of everyday life? The answer is to quiet ourselves and spend time in His presence through prayer, meditation, and reading His Word. God speaks to us in different ways—through His written Word, through the Holy Spirit, through other believers, and circumstances—but we must be attentive and open to His leading.

In John 10:27, Jesus says, "My sheep hear my voice; I know them, and they follow me." To hear His voice, we need to cultivate a heart that is willing to listen. Sometimes, this means setting aside distractions, creating space for silence, and being willing to obey, even when the direction seems unclear.

BLESSINGS IN OBEDIENCE

We may not always see immediate results when we walk in obedience, but we can trust that God is faithful. Obedience opens the door for God to work in ways that we could never have imagined. God honors our faithfulness, and though it may be challenging, it always leads to blessing.

*In **Deuteronomy 28:1-2**, God promises: "If you fully obey the Lord your God and carefully follow all his commands I give you today, the Lord your God will set you high above all the nations on earth. All these blessings will come on you and accompany you if you obey the Lord your God." Obedience to God's commands leads to blessings that exceed our expectations. It's not always about the material things but the peace, the joy, and the assurance that we are walking in His will.*

When I moved to a new place in obedience, it was not without its struggles. There were challenges—financial stress, loneliness, uncertainty— but the blessings came unexpectedly. I saw God's provision in my life, experienced a deeper connection with my children, and grew in my faith in ways I never would have if I had stayed in my comfort zone. God opened doors I didn't even know existed, and He provided not just for my physical needs but for my spiritual growth as well.

OBEYING WHEN IT'S HARD

Obedience isn't always easy. Sometimes, we don't fully understand why God is leading us in a particular direction or when the cost seems too high. But **Philippians 4:13** assures us: *"I can do all this through him who gives me strength."* When we rely on God's strength, He equips us to follow His will, even in the face of difficulties.

Obedience requires faith, and faith requires action. It's not enough to hear God's voice; we must also choose to act on it. Sometimes, the very act of obedience builds our faith and trust in God's ability to provide and guide us.

PRAYER:

Lord, I thank You for Your voice that leads me, Your Word that guides me, and Your presence that strengthens me. Help me listen attentively to You and hear Your voice above the noise of my life. Give me the courage to obey, even when it's hard, and help me to trust that Your plans for me are always good. Teach me to walk in Your will, knowing that Your blessings are found in obedience.

In Yeshua's Name (Jesus), HalleluYah and it is so !

REFLECTION QUESTIONS:

- What area of your life is God asking you to obey Him?
- How can you create space to hear God's voice more clearly?
- What blessings have you experienced in your life due to obedience?

Obedience may be challenging, but it's the path that leads us to God's greatest blessings. When we choose to listen and follow, we align ourselves with His will and experience the blessings that come from trusting Him completely.

JOURNALING:

SURRENDERING IT ALL TO GOD

"Then Jesus said to His disciples, 'Whoever wants to be My disciple must deny themselves and take up their cross and follow Me.'"
— Matthew 16:24

Surrender is one of the hardest things we are called to do, yet it is the very thing that lies at the heart of a life of faith. It's easy to say, "Lord, I trust You," but when life feels unstable—when prayers go unanswered, when suffering lingers, when heartbreak knocks at your door—true surrender is tested.

I have walked through seasons where I wanted to hold on to what I thought was best. I prayed, fasted, and tried everything possible to change my circumstances. I believed in God, but I also wanted to control the outcome. I found myself exhausted, frustrated, and questioning why things weren't happening as expected.

Then, God reminded me: *Surrender doesn't mean giving up—it means giving it to Him.*

"Trust in the Lord with all your heart, and lean not on your own understanding; in all your ways submit to Him, and He will make your paths straight."
— Proverbs 3:5-6

Surrendering is not a one-time decision; it's a daily practice. Every day, we must choose to lay down our desires, our timelines, and our expectations at the feet of Jesus. It's saying, *"Lord, even if You don't move the way I want, I will still follow You."* It's trusting that His way is better, even when we don't understand.

WHAT DOES SURRENDER LOOK LIKE?

- **Letting go of control:** We don't have to have all the answers; we just need to trust the One who does.
- **Submitting our emotions:** It's okay to feel disappointed, hurt, or confused, but we bring those emotions to God rather than letting them lead us.
- **Walking in obedience:** Even when it's hard, even when it costs us, we obey His voice and trust His direction.
- **Choosing faith over fear:** The unknown can be terrifying, but God's plans are always for our good.

"Humble yourselves, therefore, under God's mighty hand, that He may lift you up in due time. Cast all your anxiety on Him because He cares for you."

— 1 Peter 5:6-7

I won't pretend that surrender is easy. It's a battle of the flesh, a war against the desire to fix things ourselves. But every time I have truly surrendered, God has proven Himself faithful. Not always in the way I expected, but always in the way I needed.

Maybe today, you're holding on to something too tightly. A relationship, a dream, a situation that isn't unfolding as you hoped. I encourage you—let it go. Lay it down at His feet. He is a good Father, and He will not fail you.

PRAYER:

Lord, I surrender everything to You. My will, emotions, plans, and fears—I lay them all at Your feet. Help me to trust You fully, even when I don't understand. Give me the strength to let go of control and walk in faith. I believe Your way is better, and I choose to rest in that truth today.

In Yeshua's Name (Jesus), HalleluYah and it is so !

REFLECTION QUESTIONS:

- What is one thing you are struggling to surrender to God?
- How has holding on to control affected your peace?

• What would it look like to fully trust God in this season of your life?

Surrender may feel like a loss, but it is always a gain in Christ. Give it to Him and rest in His perfect plan. Here's your devotional passage on being content in all things while walking with God.

JOURNALING:

FINDING CONTENTMENT IN EVERY SEASON

"I have learned in whatever state I am, to be content."
— Philippians 4:11

There are seasons in life where everything seems to be in place—where provision, stability, and peace surround us. But then, there are also seasons of uncertainty, transition, and waiting, where we are stretched beyond our capacity. Learning to be content in every circumstance is not about pretending everything is perfect but finding peace in God, regardless of our situation.

I know what it means to trust God for provision while waiting on His timing. I left behind the comfort of my home, stepping into the unknown, simply because He said, "Go." Now, I am in a temporary living situation, adjusting to a new city, environment, and unfamiliar way of life. I could easily allow frustration, anxiety, or even regret to settle in, but I choose contentment. Not because my situation is ideal but because I know God is with me.

Contentment does not mean settling for less than God's best—it means trusting Him in the process. It means surrendering our expectations and leaning into His will, even when it doesn't make sense. It means praising Him in the temporary places, knowing He is leading us to His promises.

"But godliness with contentment is great gain."
— 1 Timothy 6:6

When Paul wrote about contentment, he was facing beatings, imprisonment, and hardships, yet he still declared that he had learned to be content. Contentment isn't rooted in circumstances—it's anchored in trust. Can we trust that God knows what He's doing? Can we trust that

He sees the bigger picture? Can we find joy even when we're in a season of waiting?

"Trust in the Lord with all your heart, and lean not on your own understanding; in all your ways acknowledge Him, and He shall direct your paths."

— Proverbs 3:5-6

Maybe you're in a season where things feel unstable, where you're longing for answers, clarity, and the fulfillment of a promise. Let me encourage you—God is faithful. He has not forgotten you. He is working behind the scenes, and even in this season, there is something to be grateful for.

Today, choose to be content. Not because everything is perfect, but because God is still good. Let your heart rest in Him, and trust that He is leading you exactly where you need to be.

In Yeshua's Name (Jesus), HalleluYah and it is so !

REFLECTION QUESTIONS:

- What is one thing you can be grateful for in this season?
- How can you shift your perspective to trust God more fully in the waiting?
- Are you allowing your current circumstances to dictate your joy, or are you choosing contentment in Christ?

No matter where you are, God is there. And in Him, you can find true contentment.

JOURNALING:

FINDING PURPOSE IN THE PAIN

"And we know that all things work together for good to those who love God, to those who are called according to His purpose."

— Romans 8:28

There were moments in my life when I questioned everything—when the weight of loss, heartbreak, and suffering seemed unbearable. I've walked through seasons where I couldn't see the purpose in my pain, where every hardship felt like another setback instead of a setup for something greater. But I've learned that God never wastes pain. Every trial, every valley, every fire we walk through is shaping us for the purpose He has ordained.

I know what it's like to be chosen. But being chosen is neither easy nor glamorous. Many desire the anointing, but few understand the crushing that often comes with it. Jesus Himself said, *"For many are called, but few are chosen."* (Matthew 22:14). Being chosen means walking a road that others may never understand. It means enduring trials that make no sense. It means standing when you feel like falling.

PAIN PRODUCES PURPOSE

Joseph was thrown into a pit by his brothers, sold into slavery, falsely accused, and imprisoned—yet all of it was a part of God's plan to lead him to his purpose (Genesis 50:20). What was meant for his harm, God used for good. Just like Joseph, our trials are not the end of our story; they are a part of our preparation.

Your pain is not in vain. That heartbreak, that betrayal, that season of isolation is molding, stretching, and refining you. The anointing comes with a cost. Before the promise, there is a process. Before the crown, there is a cross. Before the victory, there is a battle.

This is why we must never be jealous of anyone's anointing or purpose. You don't know the price they paid to walk in it. You don't know the tears they cried, the losses they endured, or the crushing they survived. You might not want to trade places if you saw what it took for them to get where they are. Instead of coveting someone else's calling, embrace the one God has specifically designed for you.

WHAT WE ENDURE PREPARES US FOR WHAT WE ARE CALLED TO

I have learned that God doesn't call the qualified; He qualifies the called. Every hardship I endured brought me closer to my calling. The pain I thought would break me became what God used to shape me. The tears I cried in secret became the prayers that strengthened me. The loss that shook me to my core deepened my dependence on Him.

"But He knows the way that I take; when He has tested me, I shall come forth as gold."

— Job 23:10

FINDING PURPOSE IN THE PROCESS

1. **Seek God First** – Purpose is not found through striving but through seeking. As you draw near to God, He will reveal your calling in His perfect timing.

"But seek first the kingdom of God and His righteousness, and all these things shall be added to you."

— Matthew 6:33

2. **Embrace the Refining Season** – The fire is painful, but it is necessary. It burns away the things that cannot go with you into your next season.
3. **Turn Your Pain into Ministry** – What you've endured can help others. Your testimony carries power, and your scars tell a story of redemption.
4. **Keep Walking in Faith** – Even when you don't understand, keep trusting. God is working behind the scenes. Your faithfulness in the valley determines your fruitfulness on the mountain.

PRAYER:

Father, I don't always understand the trials I face, but I trust that You are working everything for my good. Help me to see the purpose in my pain, to endure the refining process, and to step into the calling You have for my life. Use every hardship, every loss, and every tear for Your glory. I surrender my journey to You and ask for strength to walk boldly in faith.

In Yeshua's Name (Jesus), HalleluYah and it is so !

REFLECTION QUESTIONS:

- What trials have shaped your faith the most?
- How can you use your pain to encourage or minister to others?
- Are you allowing God to refine you, or are you resisting the process?

FINAL ENCOURAGEMENT:

If you're in the fire, know that God is refining you. If you're in the valley, know that He is guiding you. If you're in the storm, know that He is strengthening you. Your pain has a purpose, and your journey leads you to something greater. Hold on—God is not finished with your story yet.

JOURNALING:

HEALING: THE JOURNEY AND THE PROCESS

"He heals the brokenhearted and binds up their wounds."
— Psalm 147:3

Healing is a process—a journey that doesn't always look the way we want it to. It's not instant, and it often feels like two steps forward, one step back. Yet despite the setbacks, the journey can lead to wholeness, even when the scars remain. Whether we're healing from the loss of a loved one, overcoming emotional wounds, recovering from sickness, or struggling through years of hardship, the road to healing is rarely easy. But at every step, a God understands our pain, meets us where we are, and gently guides us through the process.

Loss, heartbreak, and trauma are painful realities of life. Some may feel the ache of grief after losing a child, a partner, a dream, or even a part of themselves. Others may battle past wounds, betrayal, emotional scars, or physical sickness. Healing from sickness—whether it's a chronic illness, a sudden diagnosis, or lingering pain in your body—can be just as challenging as emotional or spiritual healing. The physical pain can weigh heavy, and the battle for health can often feel isolating. But in all forms of healing, the truth remains: God is with us. He is our Healer, whether the healing comes instantaneously, over time, or in ways we never expected.

God meets us in our pain and our sickness. He doesn't expect us to have it all together, to rush through the pain, or to "just get over it." He knows the depth of our heartache and the suffering we endure physically. He sees the things we carry in secret, the ache in our bodies that no one else can see. "The Lord is near to the brokenhearted and saves the crushed in spirit." (Psalm 34:18)

God also heals our bodies. The natural world and its limitations do not limit Him. "But He was pierced for our transgressions, He was crushed for our iniquities; the punishment that brought us peace was on Him, and by His wounds, we are healed." (Isaiah 53:5). Jesus didn't just take our sins upon Himself—He also took our sicknesses and diseases. Through His sacrifice, we have access to physical healing. Healing may not always come in the way we expect; sometimes, it's a journey. But God remains faithful. He hears our cries, and He responds with mercy.

Healing often requires us to be still before God, to listen for His voice in the silence, and to allow Him to gently tend to the physical and emotional wounds that we sometimes try to ignore. **Psalm 46:10** says, *"Be still, and know that I am God."* In the stillness, we can experience the comfort of God's presence. When we stop striving to "fix" ourselves or our circumstances, God can speak healing into our hearts and bodies. But we must allow ourselves to be vulnerable before Him, to trust Him with the wounds we are carrying, and to let go of the fear of being fully seen. God does not turn away from our brokenness or our pain.

Healing is a journey, and it often involves waiting. There may be moments when we feel as though the weight of our illness or our emotional struggles will never lift. The pain may seem endless, and the longing for relief may feel overwhelming. But even in these moments, God is working. We are reminded in **Jeremiah 30:17** that, *"But I will restore you to health and heal your wounds,"* declares the Lord. Whether it's healing from grief, sickness, or emotional scars, God is a God of restoration.

As we walk this path, we must remember that healing doesn't always happen according to our timing. Sometimes healing comes gradually, and sometimes, it comes suddenly. Often, we don't understand why we must endure the pain for as long as we do. But even in the waiting, God is faithful. Even in the journey, He is working within and around us.

Healing comes when we trust in His timing and His faithfulness. It's not about instant gratification—it's about knowing that even in the midst of our pain, God is working. He is restoring, renewing, and redeeming the broken parts of our hearts and bodies.

Romans 8:28 *reminds us, "And we know that in all things God works for the good of those who love Him, who have been called according to His purpose." This means that even in our struggle for* *healing—emotional, physical, or spiritual—God works all things for our good. He is faithful, and His plans are always good.*

PRAYER:

Lord, I bring my pain, hurt, and questions to You. I am not okay and don't have all the answers, but I trust that You are with me. Heal my broken heart, bind up my wounds, and restore my body, mind, and spirit. I surrender my sickness, grief, and struggles to You, trusting that You will bring healing in Your time and in Your way. Help me to wait with patience and to rest in Your promises. I ask for Your peace to fill me as I walk this healing journey.

In Yeshua's Name (Jesus), HalleluYah and it is so !

REFLECTION QUESTIONS:

- What areas of your life—body, heart, or mind—do you need to bring to God for healing
- How can you trust in God's timing as you walk through the healing process?
- What does it look like to bring your pain and sickness to God in a raw, honest way?

Healing is a journey that may take time, but God is faithful in meeting us in the middle of our pain. God is at work, whether healing comes slowly or quickly. Trust in His process and lean into His healing touch, knowing He is making all things new.

Remember, trusting God is not about having all the answers—it's about knowing He is the answer and that He will guide us through every season of life.

- Are there areas where you've been compromising or blending in with the world?
- How can you actively pursue holiness in your thoughts, actions, and relationships?

Hold on, beloved. Your suffering is producing something greater. Joy comes in the morning.